Contents

Cats as pets   4

Which kind of cat?   6

Things you will need   8

Buying a kitten   10

Taking the kitten home   12

Play   14

Training   16

Cats outdoors   18

Feeding   20

Health care   22

Illness   24

Breeding   26

Birth and young kittens   28

Caring for your cat   30

Index   32

Cats as pets

A cat will ask to be stroked and petted, and then show its contentment by purring.

One of the nicest things about keeping a cat is that it can be let out-of-doors, and trusted to find its own way home.

It is at least four thousand years since cats were first brought into people's homes, probably to help catch mice and rats. But nowadays most cats are kept just as pets and for company.

People all over the world love cats because they are beautiful, gentle, and affectionate. They are not expensive to keep, and they are very clean: a cat spends hours grooming itself, and is easy to house-train.

An appealing thing about cats is their independent nature. Cats like to come and go as they please. They will not do what you want as a dog will. You cannot train them to do tricks or take them for walks. A cat may well ignore the bed provided for it and choose its own place to sleep. Even so, cats go out of their way to seek human company and will return every bit of affection they are given.

Looking after your
CAT

A Young Pet Owner's Guide
by Helen Piers

Text and illustrations copyright © Helen Piers 1992, 2002

First published in Great Britain in 1992
by Frances Lincoln Limited
ISBN 0-7112-0711-9

This revised edition is first published in Great Britain in 2002
by Frances Lincoln Limited, 4 Torriano Mews,
Torriano Avenue, London NW5 2RZ

www.franceslincoln.com

The author and publishers would like to thank the children
and the owners of the cats who were photographed for this book;
Sally Anne Thompson for the Siamese on p. 6; and the Cat's Protection League
and Mr A. F. Hitchins BVSc, MRCVS, of the Ark Veterinary Clinics, London, for their
help with photographs on pp. 11-12, and p. 22 and p.24 respectively. Thanks are
also due to the Fulham Pet Centre, London, and Pet Care of Chelsea, London.

The author and publishers would also like to thank Marion Hawkes, B. Vet Med, MRCVS,
of Old Courts Veterinary Centre in Brigg for checking and updating this revised edition.

British Library Cataloguing in Publication Data
available on request.

ISBN 0-7112-1921-4

Printed in Hong Kong

9 8 7 6 5 4 3 2

If you have never kept a cat before, there are a few things you will want to know before you decide whether or not to adopt a kitten.

What does it cost to keep a cat?

A cat is not expensive to keep, but you will have to buy its food, and cat litter if it uses a litter tray. There will also be the cost of vaccinations (see page 22), and perhaps some other vet's fees during its life.

Does a cat need a lot of looking after?

It needs feeding twice a day, and its litter tray emptying daily. If the family is out all day, a cat can be left by itself without being lonely. But, of course, you cannot leave it to fend for itself when you go on holiday. You will need a friend to come in twice a day to feed it, and perhaps change the litter. Alternatively, your vet may be able to recommend a good cattery where your cat can be looked after while you are away.

Only long-haired cats require frequent grooming.

A little kitten soon grows into an adult cat. Only buy a kitten if you are sure you won't get tired of it and that you will still want to look after it when it is grown up.

Are some people allergic to cats?

A few people get hay fever, asthma or skin rashes from cat hair, so keeping a cat in the same house is impossible.

Can a cat be kept indoors all the time?

If you live in a flat with no way out to a garden, try to find a kitten that has never been outside and so will not miss an outdoor life.

Which kind of cat?

A purebred (pedigree) or a mongrel?
A purebred cat is one whose ancestors are known to have been all of the same breed. A mongrel is of mixed breed, and except for its mother its ancestry is usually unknown. Most pet cats are mongrels.

Purebred kittens are expensive to buy. People often choose them because they like the looks and character of a particular breed, and with a purebred you have a better idea of what it will be like when it is grown-up. With a mongrel kitten it is not so easy to tell.

The cats on this page are some of the more common pedigree breeds. The colour of coat can vary in all breeds. On the opposite page are some typical mongrels.

Persian
Long-haired, gentle, placid, affectionate, soft musical voice

Burmese
Short-haired, sleek, athletic, brave, boisterous

Siamese
Short-haired, distinctive dark mask, ears, stockings, and tail; blue eyes, very talkative, strong personality

A male or a female?

Females stay at home more. Males like to roam about the neighbourhood, and may stay away for several days at a time when looking for a mate. Males and females can be equally affectionate.

If you have your kitten neutered, it makes little difference which sex you choose. For more information read pages 26–7.

A tortoiseshell and white (calico) cat

Long-haired or short-haired?

Long-haired cats are very beautiful, but need regular and frequent grooming to keep their coats in good condition.

A ginger (marmalade) kitten

A tabby and white cat

A black cat

Things you will need

Checklist

All kittens
- food dish
- water and milk bowls
- cat bed
- litter tray
    cat litter
    cleaning kit
- carrying box
- toys

Long-haired kittens
- grooming kit

Food dishes and milk and water bowls can be plastic or earthenware. A mat under the bowls keeps spills off the floor.

Do not buy food for the kitten until you find out which food it is used to.

A cat bed must keep out draughts and give the cat room to stretch out when fully grown. It can be plastic as shown, a wicker basket, or a bean bag.

If you do not want to buy a bed, your kitten will be just as comfortable in a cardboard box lined with newspaper and a blanket.

You will need something to bring your kitten home in, and later when you take it to the vet or on a journey. It can be a wicker basket or a specially designed cardboard carrying box, as shown, or an ordinary cardboard box with air holes punched in it and tied securely with string.

A litter tray needs to be about 30 × 40 × 9 cms deep, and made of plastic (wood soaks up moisture and harbours germs). You can buy closed-in trays or open ones, as shown. Cat litter is sold at pet shops and supermarkets.

Wear rubber gloves to handle the litter tray, and use disinfectant to clean it. The scoop is to lift out faeces.

Long-haired kittens and cats need daily grooming. You will need a cat brush and comb.

Buying a kitten

Take time choosing your kitten. One which comes up to you fearlessly may be a better choice than one – however pretty – which is too frightened to come near. These kittens were born in the cat sanctuary where their mother was taken as a stray.

You may have friends who are looking for a home for a kitten. If not, cat sanctuaries and many pet shops sell them, or you may see them advertised at the vet's surgery, in your paper shop, or in cat magazines.

If possible, buy and bring home your kitten at the weekend or during the holidays, so you do not have to leave it all alone for long during the first day or two. It may miss the company of its brothers and sisters at first.

It is best to get things ready and comfortable for your new kitten before you bring it home. You will need to plan where it is going to have its bed, and where to put the litter tray.

There are some important things to find out about the kitten you choose.

How old is it?
Between 8 and 12 weeks is best. By this age the kitten will be weaned on to solid food, and independent enough to adapt easily to its new home.

Which sex is it?

Is it healthy?
A healthy kitten is lively and playful, its *eyes* bright, clear, and not runny, its *coat* clean, glossy and without bare or thin patches. There should be no black specks or dark wax inside its *ears* – a sign of ear mites.

Has it been vaccinated?
If not, you should have this done by your vet (see page 22).

What food is the kitten used to?
Ask what food it has been given, how much and how often. You should keep to the same for the first two weeks. If you wish to change its diet later, do so gradually.

Is the kitten house-trained?
Ask if it has been using a litter tray and what kind of litter, and buy the same.

Pedigree certificate
A purebred kitten should have a certificate giving its date of birth and ancestry.

Remember
- How old is the kitten?
- Which sex is it?
- Is it healthy?
- Has it been vaccinated?
- What food is it used to, how much, and how often?
- Which cat litter is it used to?
- If it is a purebred, ask for its pedigree certificate.

Ask to hold each kitten in turn to help you decide which one you feel happiest with.

Taking the kitten home

When you get home, put the carrying box on the floor with some food and milk near by. Wait quietly for a little while before opening the box. Then lift the kitten out gently, or let it climb out when it wants to.

Make the journey home as short as possible. Rest the carrying box on your knee to prevent it jolting about, and talk soothingly to your kitten. Don't make the mistake of opening the box to look at it on the way. It might panic, leap out, and run wild in the car or train.

Your kitten will be unsettled by the journey, so it is not good to play with it too much when you first get home. Let it feel free to explore while you sit quietly and watch. It may immediately run and hide. Be patient, and wait for it to pluck up courage and come out.

It is better to keep your kitten in one room for a day or two. Let it get used to that room before you give it the run of the house.

Your kitten may be lonely during the first night because it misses its litter-mates – its brothers and sisters. You can help it to feel less alone by putting a warm hot water bottle in its bed, and perhaps a quietly ticking clock close by.

Some kittens are more nervous than others, but you will probably find your kitten will settle down in a couple of days. However, do not let it out-of-doors alone for at least a month, or it may roam too far and get lost.

The next few weeks are an important time for your kitten, when it will be getting to know and trust you. So, be gentle with it, learn how to pick it up and hold it so that it is comfortable, and don't make the mistake of expecting it to play *all* the time. Kittens sleep a lot, and there will be times when it would rather sleep than play. It will trust you more if it senses you care about how it feels.

Picking up a kitten
The correct way to pick up a kitten is to slip one hand under it, just behind its front legs, and let it sit on the other hand.

It is better not to pick it up by the scruff of the neck. Never grasp it tightly with both hands around its stomach, or grab hold of it by the tail.

Some kittens, if treated kindly and patiently, are trusting enough to sit on your shoulder and even go to sleep there.

Play

Until it is about five months old, your kitten will spend nearly all its waking time playing, and you can have great fun playing with it or just watching. Even when grown up, it will still want to play sometimes.

Cats are hunters by nature and a kitten's play is always pretend hunting or pretend fighting. Dangle anything in front of it and it will stretch out a paw and try to catch it. It will bring its toys to life by patting or tossing them about so it can stalk and chase them. It will lie on its back kicking and 'fighting' with a duster.

You can give your kitten cotton reels to play with, old soft toys, paper screwed into balls, or scrumpled newspaper. And it is sure to find other toys for itself! See that it doesn't play with anything sharp, or small enough to swallow. Be very careful it doesn't get hold of wool or cotton with a needle attached.

If your kitten gets its claws caught in your clothes or some other material and cannot get them out, help it by gently unhooking them.

Training

Your kitten should be trained while it is still young to behave the way you want it to, because it is hard to change the habits of an adult cat.

A kitten cannot know when it is doing something wrong, and will not understand if it is punished, so it is important to remember you are not punishing your kitten, only teaching it good habits.

Training a kitten not to go in forbidden places
There may be rooms in which your kitten is not allowed, or cupboards where it could get shut in by mistake. It may want to jump up on tables where there is food. It has to learn that these places are out of bounds.

The way to teach it is to pick it up *at once* every time it goes where it is not allowed. Hiss, and say 'No!' firmly. Don't overdo it. You don't want to *scare* the kitten — only alarm it a little, so that it learns to dislike that place. It should feel that though you are not pleased, inside you still feel kind towards it.

A scratching post can be made by wrapping a piece of carpet around a wooden post (60–90 cm high), which is then nailed to a heavy base to steady it. Or you can simply nail a piece of carpet firmly to the wall.

Clawing furniture
In the same way you can train your kitten not to claw and spoil furniture and carpets. However, to keep their claws in good condition, all cats do need something to scratch on. The best thing is to train them to use a scratching post.

16

Training a kitten to use a litter tray

Your kitten has to learn that the litter tray is the only place in which it is allowed to wet or mess. So, if it begins to puddle or mess anywhere else, pick it up *at once.* Hiss, and take it to the tray.

If it has already made a mess, after washing the dirty place, it is a good idea to spray it with vinegar to cover up any smell, or the kitten will go back and use it again.

If you want your kitten to wet and mess outdoors when it is older, mix earth with the cat litter and keep the tray by the garden door. When your kitten is allowed out on its own, move the litter tray outside, and keep it there until the kitten finds places in the garden to use instead.

Remember

● Be consistent. Don't stop your kitten jumping on a table one day, and let it the next.
● Don't slap it. It won't understand, and you might harm it.
● Don't discipline your kitten *after* it is naughty. Try to catch it in the act.
● A cat won't use a dirty litter tray. Faeces should be scooped out as soon as found. The litter tray needs washing with disinfectant *once a week*, then rinsing well.
● Wear rubber gloves when cleaning the litter tray – cat excreta has germs in it.

The kitten will prefer the litter tray to be in a corner or under a shelf or table. Cats instinctively need to feel protected and private when using the tray, because if living wild they would be more open to attack by enemies at this time.

Cats outdoors

Some cats climb trees and spend hours stalking birds. Pet cats are not always successful hunters, but if yours does proudly bring you a bird it has caught, try not to be cross. It is a natural instinct for a cat to hunt, and by bringing you the bird, your cat is showing that it feels a real family bond with you.

Cats have the best of two worlds. Indoors they enjoy comfort and human company, and outdoors they can do things which are natural for a wild cat to do – hunting, defending their territory and basking in the sun.

Fighting

Toms will fight over a female, but most cat fights are territorial. Cats mark out their own piece of the neighbourhood, and defend it fiercely. The best way to break up a fight is to clap and make a lot of noise.

Danger from traffic

Try to train your kitten to stay in the back garden, so it gets in the habit of never going near the road and risking being run over.

Straying

Cats do sometimes lose their bearings and are unable to find their way home. If your cat goes missing, put up 'Lost' notices around the neighbourhood and make enquiries at any local animal welfare organizations. Don't give up hope. Cats have been found after being missing for some months.

It is a good idea to put a collar on your cat with an address disc attached. The collar must have a piece of elastic set into it so the cat can wriggle out of it should it get caught on something.

Cats love basking in the sun. Your cat will choose its own favourite places for sunbathing.

You can fit a special cat flap in the garden door so that your cat can come in and out when it likes.

Feeding

Many cats enjoy milk although some will get an upset tummy from it, in which case it is best to give special 'cat milk'. Ensure that fresh water is always available, even if your cat does not seem to drink it very much.

Cats are carnivorous so they must be fed meat and fish-based diets. These can be canned, dry or, as a treat, fresh food.

Canned Food

Feeding your cat on canned food is the safest way to make sure it has a healthy diet, because canned foods are specially prepared to provide the right amounts of protein, fat, vitamins and minerals a cat needs.

Dry Food

These can help keep teeth clean if fed regularly. A cat on a diet of dry food *must drink at least* one cupful of water, milk or gravy a day, or it may develop serious bladder problems. Your vet can recommend a suitable brand for your cat. Always make sure your cat has plenty of water available.

Fresh Food

Chicken, turkey, beef, lamb, rabbit and most kinds of fish can be given as a treat. The meat and fish should be cooked, cut up, minced or flaked, and the bones removed. Avoid fish like herring, which have very fine bones.

How much food and how often

Follow the chart below, which is also a guide for weaning a kitten. The amounts of food are only approximate, because appetites vary depending on size and how much exercise your cat takes. If it never eats what you put down for it within a half an hour, begin to give less. A cat will ask for more if hungry.

While the kittens are still with their mother and having her milk, at four weeks old kittens can be offered a little canned kitten food. If ever it is necessary to supplement the mother's milk, you can give special kitten milk or three parts unsweetened evaporated milk to one part boiled water. Both may be thickened with a little baby cereal food for extra nourishment. Never give cow's milk to kittens. They can leave their mother when they are eight weeks old when they will no longer need her milk.

Remember

- Give a variety of foods.
- Don't let your kitten get too choosy and eat only the food it likes best.
- Take away food not eaten in a half an hour, and give less at next mealtime.
- Make sure you leave water down at all times.
- Never give canned dog food.

Feeding chart

Age	Feeds for one day	Approx. amount needed daily	
		Canned	Dry*
4 to 8 weeks	4–5 (and mother's milk)	Up to 3 tbsp	0
8 to 12 weeks	4–5	4 tbsp	1–2 tbsp
12 to 24 weeks	3–4	5 tbsp	2.5–3 tbsp
up to 10 months	2–3	6 tbsp	4 tbsp
after 10 months	2	6–8 tbsp	4.5–5 tbsp

* Measurments are approximate. Please check the manufacturer's instructions.

Health care

You will have to take your kitten to a veterinary surgeon to be vaccinated. The injection may be painful for the kitten just for a moment, but it will not feel ill afterwards.

Cats usually enjoy good health, but there are a few things you should do to prevent your cat getting ill, and to make sure it is in really good condition.

Vaccination
Your kitten must be vaccinated against cat flu and other serious illnesses at two months old. It needs two shots a few weeks apart, plus an annual booster.

Treatment for fleas
De-flea your cat or kitten regularly whether or not you think it has fleas. The vet or pet shop will give you a treatment to use on your cat, and another for its bedding.

Treatment for worms
Worms are small parasites, which can live inside a cat's intestines. They do not cause serious illness, except in small kittens, but a cat with worms cannot be really well. It will always be hungry. It may be thin or have diarrhoea and vomit. Kittens and cats need regular de-worming. The vet will give you the necessary tablets.

Checking for ear mites
Examine your cat's ears regularly. If you can see any dark brown wax or crusty material inside, this could be ear-mites, and you should consult your vet.

Grooming

A *short-haired* cat does not really need grooming, but an occasional gentle brushing gets rid of loose hairs, and keeps its skin healthy. And the cat loves it!

A *long-haired* cat needs brushing and combing regularly – daily if possible. Apart from caring for the cat's coat, this prevents it swallowing too many hairs when washing itself. These form *hairballs*, which, if it cannot cough them up, may cause a blockage in its stomach. If your cat starts developing hairballs frequently, you should consult your vet.

Bathing a cat is rarely necessary. If you do have to bath your cat use a mild shampoo. Be as quick as possible, and keep the cat in the warm afterwards so it does not catch cold.

A long-haired cat enjoys a daily grooming. Tangles can be teased out with a comb, and matted hairs cut away with *blunt-ended* scissors.

A short-haired cat should be brushed the way the hair grows. Brush a long-haired cat the opposite way, to fluff up the hair.

Cats are very particular about keeping clean, and kittens learn to groom themselves and each other from an early age.

Illness

How do you know if your cat is ill?

There are different signs or symptoms which show a cat is not well (see opposite). But one symptom alone does not necessarily mean the cat is seriously ill. For example, it could vomit, but if otherwise well, then it may only have eaten something which did not agree with it.

Watch your cat carefully. If the symptoms get worse, or go on for more than a day, or if the cat seems miserable and begins to show other symptoms, *then take it to the vet at once.*

People sometimes put off taking their cat to the vet because they are afraid of what it will cost. It is well worth taking out insurance for your cat, to help cover the vet's fees.

The vet will find out what is wrong with your cat, then give you medicine for it, and tell you how to care for it.

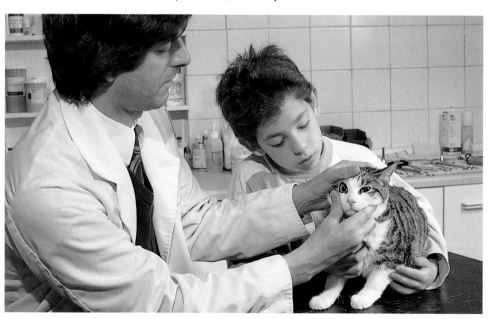

24

If your cat is wounded in a fight and the wound is not bad enough to need stitches, you can clean it by bathing it in warm water (boiled and allowed to cool) with a drop of mild antiseptic added to it. But if the wound gets at all inflamed then take your cat to the vet.

Apart from caring for minor wounds, never try to treat your cat yourself. A sick animal cannot tell you how it feels, and only a veterinary surgeon has the skill and knowledge to find out what is really wrong. And never give a cat medicines meant for people. It is dangerous. Aspirin, for example, can cause a cat's death.

Serious illness

Like any other animal, a cat may develop some illness which cannot be cured. If this should happen, your vet may ask if you wish him to put it down – end its life painlessly. This will be a very sad and difficult decision for you. But no vet likes putting an animal down, and will only suggest it to save your cat suffering and pain, and only if there is no hope of curing it.

Signs of illness

- eating less, or nothing at all
- drinking more than usual
- vomiting (being sick)
- diarrhoea
- straining when using litter tray
- a dull and 'spiky' coat
- difficulty in breathing
- dull or runny eyes
- runny nose
- not bothering to groom itself

Breeding

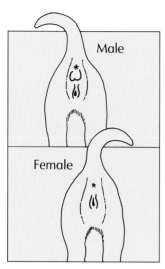

Male

Female

Sexing a kitten
If you lift the kitten's tail you will see there are two openings. The one closest to the tail is the anus. In a *male* the second opening is 1 cm away and separated by two darkish raised areas, which are the scrotal sacs. In the *female* it is a narrow slit almost joining the anus. Male cats are called *toms*, and females *queens*.

It is important to decide before your kitten is five months old whether you want it to mate when it is grown up, and parent kittens, or whether to have it neutered.

Neutering involves a small operation by the vet, from which the cat recovers quickly. Neutering a male cat is called *castrating*, and a female, *spaying*. Apart from its no longer wanting to mate, these operations do not change a cat's character.

The problem with an unneutered male is that it may roam far afield looking for a mate, and so run more risk of getting lost or run over. Its litter tray too – if it uses one – may smell unpleasant. An unneutered male can parent hundreds of kittens in its lifetime, not all of which will be wanted.

An unneutered female, when she is in season (the only time she can become pregnant – about three times a year) is restless and howls, 'calling' for a mate. You would probably like your cat to have kittens, but if she has more than one litter every year it may be difficult to find homes for so many kittens. It is possible for a female cat to have one or two litters before she is spayed.

If you decide not to neuter your female cat she will choose a mate from among the neighbourhood cats. While mating she will stay out for a day or two, and not come in even to eat. If you have never seen cats mating before, the male may seem to be attacking her, but he is not. She will squeal and spit at him. Don't worry. This is normal mating behaviour, and she will come away when she wants to.

It is kinder to neuter a housebound cat which will have no opportunity to mate.

The main reason for neutering cats is to avoid many unwanted kittens being born.

Mating a pedigree

Should you want your pedigree cat to have purebred kittens you will need to find her a mate of the same breed *before* she comes into season. Breeders advertise in cat magazines when they have a *stud* (tom suitable for breeding). Or you can write to her breed club (see page 31).

If you want your pedigree cat to have purebred kittens (these are Persian), then you must not let her out-of-doors when she is in season, or she will mate with a mongrel tom, and her kittens will not be pedigrees.

Birth and young kittens

A kittening box should be deep enough to keep out draughts and prevent the kittens tumbling out. It is a mistake to put in a cushion. Newspaper or a washable towel or blanket is enough. When she gives birth, the mother will prefer the bottom of the box to be soft, but firm.

This cardboard box has a hole cut in it for the mother to climb in and out, and when you want to look at the kittens you can lift up the flaps.

Your cat will be pregnant for nine weeks. She will not need special care, though she will be hungry, and eat more than usual. If this is her first litter, it is sensible to take her to the vet for a check-up about a week before the kittens should be born. At the same visit, the vet will give you advice about the birth.

About two weeks before the kittens are due, the mother will begin to look for a place to give birth to them. So keep cupboards and drawers shut! Put a few cardboard boxes in quiet, warm places for her to choose from instead, and line them with newspaper and blankets to tempt her.

The birth

Most cats have no trouble giving birth, and prefer to be alone. But your cat may want someone there to give her confidence, though she will still know instinctively what to do, and will not need help. If at any time you feel she is in real trouble, you should phone the vet.

The kittens will be born one at a time, each in its own bag of membrane (thin, transparent skin), which the mother will remove. She will then lick each kitten clean, before the next is born. Soon all her kittens will be lying in a neat line, each sucking milk from one of her teats, and she will be purring happily. Show her you are pleased, but don't touch the kittens. Just give her a bowl of milk, and then leave her to be quiet and peaceful.

At first the kittens will feed only on their mother's milk. She will not need help with them, though she will want more than twice as much food herself, as well as vitamins and calcim supplements – obtainable from the vet or pet shops.

When the kittens are *two days* old begin to stroke them gently, with just one finger.

At *two weeks* lift each kitten out and hold them for a few minutes each day.

At *four weeks*, when the kittens begin to explore outside their box, you can have fun playing with them freely, and begin to wean them on to solid food (see page 21). This is also the time to put down a litter tray, and to advertise for homes for them.

At *eight weeks* the kittens should be weaned and ready to go to their new homes.

Remember

- Do handle the kittens from an early age.
- Don't play with each one for more than five minutes at a time until they leave the box.
- Change or wash the blanket under the kittens frequently.
- Don't de-flea or worm the kittens or mother without first consulting the vet.
- Let the mother keep at least one kitten until it is ten or more weeks old.
- Don't take all the kittens from her on the same day.

At some time, a mother may move her kittens to another place. She may decide it is noisy downstairs, and take them to a bedroom. She will carry them there one at a time. If she chooses somewhere unsuitable, don't fluster her. Let her move all the kittens before you persuade her to settle in a better place.

Caring for your cat

Your cat will give you hours of pleasure and companionship throughout its life. A cat may be independent and like to come and go as it pleases, but even so it becomes very attached to its home and its owner, and needs every bit of affection and understanding you can give it.

Useful Information

Length of Pregnancy	9 weeks
Number of kittens in a litter	1–6
Number of litters a female cat can have in one year	2–4
Kitten's eyes open at	10-14 days
Age to start weaning	4 weeks
Age to finish weaning	8 weeks
First vaccination	8 weeks
Age to leave mother	8–12 weeks
Best age to neuter	5 months
Males can mate at	6–8 months
Females can mate at	5 months
Best age for a female to have her first litter	18 months
Fully grown at	9–12 months
Average length of life	14 years

Further reading

Care for your cat
RSPCA Pet Guide
Collins, 1990

Care for your kitten
RSPCA Pet Guide
Collins, 1990

Cat and Kittens
Katherine Starke
Osborne, 1998

Caring for your cat
AngelaGair
(In association with the Cats'
Protection League)
Harper Collins, 1997

Useful addresses

Cats' Protection League
17 King's Road, Horsham, West Sussex

RSPCA Headquarters
The Manor House, Horsham, West Sussex, RH12 1HG

Governing Council of the Cat Fancy (GCCF) Headquarters
4-6 Penel Orlieu, Bridgewater, Somerset, TA6 3PG

You can get addresses of individual breed clubs from the GCCF or by looking in the GCCF Directory in a library.

Index

A
Address disc 19
Allergy, to cat hair 5

B
Bed 8, 12
Burmese 6
Birth 28
Buying a kitten 10

C
Carrying box 8, 9
Cat flap 19
Cat litter 5, 8, 11
Cereal, for kittens 21
Clawing furniture 16
Cleaning litter tray 5, 8, 9, 17
Collar 19
Cost, of keeping a cat 5

E
Ear mites 11, 22

F
Fighting 18
Fleas 22
Feeding 5, 11, 20, 21
Food dishes 8

G
Grooming 4, 5, 8, 9, 23

H
Hairballs 23
Health, signs of good 11
Health care 22
Holidays 5
House-training 4, 11, 17
Hunting 18

I
Illness 24–25
Insurance 24

L
Litter, of kittens 26, 31
Litter tray 5, 8, 9, 11, 17
Long-haired cats 5, 6, 7, 23
Length of life 31

M
Mating 26, 27, 31
Meat, for kittens 21
Milk 20
    for kittens 21

N
Neutering 7, 26, 27, 31

P
Pedigree cats 6, 11, 27
Persian 6, 27
Picking up, how 13

S
Sanctuary, for cats 10
Scratching post 16
Sexing, of kittens 26
Short-haired cats 7, 23
Siamese 6
Straying 19
Stud 27

T
Toys 8, 14–15
Traffic, danger from 19

V
Vaccination 5, 22
Veterinary surgeon 5, 22, 24, 25

W
Water 20
Weaning 21, 29, 31
Worms 22
Wounds 25